Exploration of Comptia Security+

Exam Guide SY0-401

By Alfred Quinn

Table of contents

Introduction   **5**
Chapter 1- Network Security   **6**
Network Security Implementation Mechanisms   13
Attacker Tools   18
Port scanners   18
Network Sniffers   18
Vulnerability scanners   19
Password crackers   20
Chapter 2- Compliance and Operation Security   **21**
Operational Security Measures   21
Defence in Depth   24
Complexity and Security   25
Regulation and Compliance   25
Chapter 3- Data, Application, and Host Security   **26**
Data Security   26
Host Security   29
Brute Force Compromise   31
Viruses and Malware   31
Application Security Measures   32
Chapter 4- Identity Management   **35**
Chapter 5- Cryptography   **37**
Components of Cryptography   37
Message Digest Functions   37
Digital Signatures   39
Secret Key Exchange   39
Encryption   39
Hashed Message Authentication   39
Conclusion   **40**

Introduction

Every organization has some sensitive or private information which they never wish to disclose to the public, enemies, or competitors. Such information should be kept securely at all times to prevent it from getting into the hands of unauthorized personnel. For this to be case, the network, the hosts, and the applications of the organization has to be adequately secured. There are several mechanisms which can be employed to ensure that this happens. These are all discussed in this guide, thus, you will learn how to implement them in your organization. Enjoy reading!

Chapter 1- Network Security

Network security is a special field in computer networking which deals with the securing of the network infrastructure of a computer. This job is usually done by a systems administrator or a network administrator, and these are tasked with implementation of the necessary network software, network hardware, and security policy to protect the network and its resources from attacks. They are also responsible for ensuring that the employees of the organization can adequately access the network and its resources which are necessary for them to work.

The security system of a network relies on layers of protection, and has multiple components such as security software and networking monitoring, hardware, and other appliances. All these components coordinate their efforts so that the security of the network can be greatly improved.

Sources and Types of Network Threats

There are several types of network threats. There are also various mechanisms which can be used for the protection of a computer network against these types of threats. We will discuss these in this section.

1. Denial-of-service

Denial-of-service (DOS) attacks are the most prevalent types of attacks, and the most difficult for us to address. They are very easy for hackers to launch, and very hard to track or detect.

The mechanism behind this type of network attack is very simple. More requests are sent to a particular machine until they exceed the number of requests that it can handle. A number of tool kits will usually run in the background, which makes the work of the running program easy by telling it the host to which it should launch attacks. The program used by the attacker uses a service port to establish a connection, and this is mostly done by forging the header information of a packet which specifies the origin and destination of a packet. It then drops the connection. If the host has the capability of servicing 30 requests per second, and then the attacker sends it 60 requests per second, then it will become hard for the host to service all of those requests. The following are some measures which can help you to protect your network from a denial-of-service attack:

• Avoiding running servers which are visible-to-the-world close to their capacity.
• Applying packet filtering for prevention of forged packets getting into the network space. Forged packets will also claim to be coming from your own host, the addresses which have been reserved for the private network and the loop back network.
• Staying up-to-date on patches related to security on the operating system of your host.

2. Unauthorized access

This term can be used for the purpose of referring to different forms of network attacks. The attack is aimed at accessing a resource which your machine is not expected to provide the attacker with.

An example of such a case is when a web server is the host, and it should not provide the attacker with the requested web pages. If the host is granting access to the shell, it should not do so unless it is very sure that the party is authorized to access the shell, like a local administrator.

3. Executing Commands Illicitly

It occurs that an entrusted party gains access and executes commands on your system, and especially the server machines. These types of access are classified into two categories based on the level of their severity: the normal user access and the administrator access. There are some tasks that a normal user should do once they have accessed the system which an attacker should not be able to do. Examples of such tasks include reading files and mailing them to other users. An attacker might wish to carry out these tasks in your system, and once they gain access into it, they will do it. Sometimes, the attacker might be in need of making some configuration changes to your system, such as changing the IP address of the server, changing the start-up script to shut down your machine once started, and similar actions. For this to be done, the attacker should gain administrative access into your system.
Confidentiality breaches
You might be aware of the thread model. What do you need to protect yourself against? You might have some information which might ruin you if it falls into the hands of your competitor, enemy, or the public. In such a case, compromising the user account on your local machine is enough to cause you damage, such as through PR or by getting information which can simply be used to bring down your company.

4. Destructive behavior

Destructive attacks are classified into two categories:

• Data diddling - this is the very worse attack due to the fact that an immediate break-in might not be easily detected. The attacker may be changing the dates which are contained in your plan or projections, or the numbers contained in your spreadsheets. The account numbers might be changed for the purpose of auto-depositing some certain paychecks. You will just come to work as usual, and rarely will you realize that something has gone wrong. When auditing is done, most probably sometime after the act, you will then realize that there are discrepancies. Tracking the problem which occurred will be difficult for you, and no member will trust because it has taken a long period.

• Data destruction - some individuals who perpetrate attacks only wish to delete some things. In such a case, the impact will be too severe for your business, like a fire which comes to destroy anything, or after occurrence of an earthquake in which the computing machines may be destroyed completely.

Types of Malicious Software

The following are some classes of malicious software:

1. Viruses - this is form of a program which propagates itself by attaching itself to another program to become part of it. It then travels from one computer to another, and in the process, it leaves each computer infected. The severity of these virus attacks can be mild or severe, ranging from changing the files to damaging them or causing a denial-of-service. In most cases, the virus attaches itself to an executable file, meaning that the virus can stay inactive until the user executes or opens that file. Once the host code has been executed, the viral code will also be executed. What happens is that the host will continue to function even after an attack by the virus.

2. Worms - computer worms are just like viruses in that they work by replicating functional copies of their own, and they have the capability of causing similar damage. As we said earlier, viruses need a host program so that they can perform replication and spreading. However, this is different with worms, as they are independent, and they spread on their own, without the need to attach themselves to a host program. Worms usually spread by tricking the user to execute them or by taking advantage of a vulnerability of the system.

3. Trojans - this is harmful software which looks as though it were useful to the user. It works by tricking the user into executing it, thinking that it will be of help. Once it has been executed, it affects the system in a number of ways, such as damaging the host and its files, irritating the user by changing the desktop or by pop-up windows. It can damage data and steal data in the same way that viruses operate. Trojans also have a unique functionality in which they create a backdoor, and this is used for attackers to attack the network system. Reproduction of the Trojan is not done by infection of other files nor through self-replication. They have to be spread through mechanisms involving interaction with the user such as downloading of a file from the Internet and then executing it, or by downloading an e-mail attachment and then opening it on your system.

4. Bots - this is an automated process which interacts with other services of the network. These usually automate tasks and perform the tasks which required a human being to carry out. They are commonly used for gathering information or for interaction with web interfaces. They can also be used for the purpose of a dynamic interaction with other websites.

A malicious bot will infect a system and then establish a connection to a central server which then serves as the command and central server.

How are they carried out?

Most people wonder how an attacker can gain access into a system. Connections which you have established to the outside world are used for an attacker to gain access into the equipment. Examples of these include dial-up modems, Internet connections, and even the physical address.

For you to ensure that your network is completely secured, all mechanisms of gaining access into network have to be identified and then evaluated. The security of each of those entry mechanisms should be identified well.

Network Security Implementation Mechanisms

There are a number of high-level mechanisms which can be used for prevention of network security disasters. These can also be used for prevention of damages in any case in which the preventive measures have failed to thwart the attacks. Let us discuss some mechanisms which can help us prevent network attacks:

1. Backups - in terms of security, this may not be a good idea. The operational requirements should be capable of defining the backup policy, and this should work together with the plan for disaster recovery, such that if something wrong affects your system, you will be in a position to continue providing service to your customers. Backups are one of the ways to ensure that there is fault tolerance in your system. Also, disasters do occur and with a backup system, it will be easy for to perform a recovery or in other occurrences in which your data has been damaged.

2. Putting data in the necessary location
This is very essential, as it is one of the ways of ensuring that the data does not get into wrong hands such as your competitors, enemies, or the public. If the information is not supposed to be accessed from the outside world, make sure that you keep it in a place which has been well secured, and this will help protect your data.

3. No use of Single point of failure systems
If your security system can be compromised only by breaking into a single component, then it will not be strong enough. Redundancy is very good for us to ensure that we have a string security system, and this can help protect your organization from a security breach which might have caused a disaster in your organization.

4. Firewalls
This is the most common security measure nowadays. The firewall is any perimeter mechanism which can help in permitting or denying traffic based on some set of rules which have been defined by the network administrator. This means that the firewall can even be a router having some access lists or a set of some modules which have been distributed throughout your network, and their control is from a single location.

It serves to protect the network from both behind and from the front. The front of a firewall is regarded as the Internet which is facing it, while the back of the firewall is the internal network The firewall has been designed in such a way that it will be in a position to protect the various types of networks, which is usually referred to as the firewall topology.

There are certain packages which you can use in your desktop machine and make it invisible to pings and other types of network probes. Some will also allow you to permit and deny your resources from accessing the Internet. This will mean that you will be in a position to allow your mail client and the browser to access the Internet, but deny any suspicious program from accessing the Internet if that is your choice. With this kind of protection, you will be in a great position to protect your network from attacks by worms and a Trojan horse.

However, you should be aware that a firewall is just a set of rules. This means that you cannot rely on it alone as a means of protecting your network from attacks. There are several mechanisms which attackers can use to identify weaknesses, faults, and errors in your firewall and this will allow them to gain unauthorized access into your network. In the majority of firewalls, most traffic is blocked except the one from port 53 (DNS, the domain name server). This one will allow the client machines to resolve host names into IP addresses. An attacker can take advantage of this rule to gain unauthorized access into your network, and the security of the network will have been compromised. They can easily change the source port of their attack to 53, and the firewall will assume that the traffic is from DNS, which is not the case.

Some attackers will even bypass the firewall to gain access into your network.

5. Antivirus systems

Most people, even non-IT professionals, are very aware of desktop versions of antivirus. These operate in a very simple policy, such that once the researchers have identified a new virus, they just have to write its signature after determining its whole characteristics. The whole load of the signatures which are to be scanned by the antivirus is referred to as the "virus definitions."

This explains the reason as to why your anti-virus should be kept up-to-date. However, it is good that most antivirus mechanisms have an automatic way of doing it. If you have an organization, it will be good for you to install an antivirus program in all of your computers, but a policy doesn't exist on the regular update of the definitions.

E-mail viruses have spread and are spreading at a very high rate. This calls for use of an anti-virus program at the email server, which is very good. What happens with this is that email server will scan any emails that it receives for viruses, and implement the necessary quarantine measures if necessary. You have to know that all mails have to pass to the mail server, which means that it is the central point in which scanning for viruses can be done. Most mail servers are always connected to the Internet, meaning that they will regularly download the latest definitions for their antivirus programs. Antivirus alerts are always common. There is a need for us to train end users on how to respond to these. If one user in the organization opens an infected file, then it will spread throughout the organization.

6. Intrusion-detection systems

These are classified into two types:

- Host-based IDS
- Network-based IDS

The Host-based IDS systems have to be installed on a particular machine, most probably the server machine or a target machine, and this is tasked with ensuring that the state of the system matches what has been set in the baseline. An example is when a change is made to a particular file, and in such a case, the administrator has to be alerted about it. This is of great importance, as most network attackers will need to replace a system file with a Trojan file so that they can gain backdoor access into your network and the system.

Network-based IDS systems are very popular, and at the same time much easier for installation.

They are made up of the common network sniffer which runs, meaning that the network card will be picking all the traffic even that which is not meant for it.

The sniffer has to be connected to a database which has the commonly known attack signatures, and it has to analyse each packet it receives to identify any form of attacks.

This means that there must be an ID in the packet which when it matches the one contained in the database, the packet will be considered to be infected with a virus and then discarded, or any other necessary measure applied.

The problem with the IDS system is that it generates numerous false positives. This is just a false alarm, in which case the sniffer will detect a legitimate pattern and then match it to an attack signature contained in the database. These will tempt the administrator to turn them off, or in some cases, he will not even bother to read the logs. This can then lead into an actual attack occurring.

In the case of experienced attackers, they use a mechanism known as ID evasion. This is done by modifying the attack in such a way that the signature will not be identified. In most cases, the attack signature is written in a hexadecimal format, which means that the ID will be evaded. Again, the attacker may choose to distribute the attack by fragmenting the packets.

In this case, each packet will have a small part of the ID, meaning that the ID contained in the administrator's database will not be matched. Some IDs have the capability of assembling these packets. However, the problem comes in that some packets are dropped in the event of processing, meaning that the whole of the attacker's ID will not be assembled.

The good thing with network-based IDs is that detection by an attacker becomes very hard. Most of these IDs are not expected to generate any traffic, and most of them make use of a broken TCP/IP stack, meaning that they lack an IP address. This will mean the attacker will not be aware of whether the network segment is under surveillance or not.

7. Patching and Segmenting

Although you may not see it as part of a security measure, it is. The mechanism is greatly used for stopping an attack. However, the level of patching which is done is still inadequate. Before an attack can be detected, it can take a long period, and many hosts will have already been infected.

In a majority of today's organizations, the lack mechanisms by which patching can be applied to a many machines, but some mechanisms have been implemented which make the burden somehow easier for us.

Attacker Tools

There are the tools which are commonly used by network attackers. The funny thing is that most of these tools are the ones which are available in the common operating systems. Examples of such tools include the ping and trace route.

Port scanners

Any system with the capability of offering UDP or TCP will have a port left open for that purpose. If your machine is serving web pages, the TCP port 80 will be left open.

A port scanner works by scanning a system to know the ports which have been left open and the kind of tasks which are being run on those ports. This gives the attacker and hint about the systems which can be attacked. Consider a situation in which the attacker scans your server and then finds that the port 80 is being used for running an old web server. I can then use a collection of exploits to attack the system. Port scanning is always done during the earliest stages of an attack which is a mechanism for the attacker to determine the target hosts.

This is done for the user to survey the network properly, to know the kind of services offered in the network, and the operating systems which are being used. Nmap is a good example of a port scanner. This tool is very versatile, and runs on almost all operating systems, and it has many features such as stealth scanning, service version scanning, and OS fingerprinting. Superscan is also another popular scanner, but this only runs on the Windows platform.

Network Sniffers

This works by putting the Network Interface Card (NIC) of a computer into its promiscuous mode. In this type of mode, the NIC will pick up all the traffic regardless of whether the traffic was meant for it or not. Attackers will usually layup network sniffers so that they can capture all the traffic on the network and get to know about the login details such as usernames and passwords. TCPdumb is the most popular type of network sniffer. This one can be run on the command line, which is what most attackers use. Iris and Ethereal are the other popular types of network sniffers.

If we have a switched network as our target network, a normal network scanner will not help in any way. In such occurrences, we are expected to use sniffer Ettercap for the switched network. With this tool, the attacker will find it easy to hijack sessions, collect passwords, kill connections, and modify the connections which are outgoing. Secured communications such as SSL (Secure Socket Layer) can also be sniffed.

Network admins should make use of the necessary tools to determine whether their NICs are running in the promiscuous mode.

Vulnerability scanners

This can be seen to work in the same way as a port scanner. After identification of the services which are running, it will check the system against a huge database having known vulnerabilities, and then a report will be prepared which will specify all the security holes which will have been found.

This calls for updating of the software to scan for any latest security holes. It is easy for anyone to use these tools, so most attackers will point them at the target machine so that they can determine any loopholes which can be used for attacking. GFI LanScan and Retina are the most common types of such tools. Network administrators should also take advantage of such tools to scan their network and identify the holes which might exist within their system.

Password crackers

Password cracking involves the following two modes:

• Dictionary mode - this involves the attacker feeding the password cracker with some common passwords such as "XYZ," "123," and the rest. The cracker tries each of the passwords to check whether there is a match. The attack is very important when the attacker has some information regarding the target. An example is when I know that you have used the name of game as the password. I can just get a dictionary and try all the names of games which I find.

In most cases, the attacker has a large collection of lists of words. They are very aware of the words which most people use as passwords, such as birth date, name, phone number, and others. This is why using such as the password is not recommended at all. Some people think that they can use their names as passwords and then add some numbers at the end. This is not secure, as some password crackers have the capability of adding numbers at the end of the words they have in the list.

• Brute force mode - this involves the cracker trying all the possible combinations for the password. Any possible password has to be guessed, but the mechanism takes too much time. Although you might see this as impossible, you might wonder when it gets it right since modern computers are very powerful. Suppose that you have used a five or maybe 6 alphanumeric passwords. Depending on the power of your hardware and software, this can be cracked in just a few hours or days. l0phtcrack for Windows and the Unix John the Ripper are examples of some powerful password crackers.

Chapter 2- Compliance and Operation Security

The security of a network is dependent on three factors, each independent of each other.

These include the following:

1. Architecture (or the algorithm) which has been set in place.
2. Implementation of the algorithm or the architecture. This is used for describing how the implementation of the algorithm or the architecture has been done. Mistakes made programmatically, such as the buffer overflows, can affect this.
3. Operation - these are the operator issues, such as selecting weak passwords on your workstations and routers, or accidentally disclosing a shared key. An example is when the configurations have been sent to the wrong parties.

The severity of misconfigurations differs, ranging from mild to catastrophic. However, it is good for you to know that even with misconfigurations, only a fraction of them will result into a breach of security. However, with deliberate misconfigurations, there is a high chance that a breach in security will occur since it was done deliberately.

Operational Security Measures

Whenever you are facing a security problem, the best solution is for you to look for the necessary configuration and then do the configuration. You should note that operational problems cannot be fully settled using features, since the individual who had been made the misconfiguration may also do away with the feature once it has been added. The following are some operational solutions:

1. Operational security policy - guidelines should be specified to dictate what the operators should do and what they should not do. One also needs to define the operation paths which will dictate the steps which should be followed in case the operator lacks the authorization which is required for a specified action to be carried out. This policy should specify the authorization and responsibilities, and the disciplinary actions which should be taken in case a security breach occurs. The policy should also operate to prevent the users from doing deliberate misconfigurations.

2. Change management process - this policy dictates how changes to the network which have been laid out should be made. Monitoring should be done on the state of the hardware, software, and configurations and any changes should be made in a controlled way and then logged. The logs have to be evaluated and then checking done for any potential misconfigurations. These are necessary, as they can reveal any deliberate misconfiguration or violation of the policy.

3. Access control - it is recommended that one should restrict how network devices are being assessed. In most networks, access control policies are implemented by use of the AAA authorizations. In most cases, this security measure has to be executed for a device to access a network resource, but most of the operators will have access to the network devices. For you to take care of the risk, one has to reduce the number to the minimum amount of operators.

4. Authorization - the operator has an access which has to be restricted to the minimum access which is needed so that the operator can do its job. It is not good for all the available operators to be granted access to the devices which are available. Although this type of implementation can be a bit difficult, it is still possible to be implemented, such as by defining who is allowed to enter the configuration mode.

5. Dual control - the process of securing the network and implementing the security policies should not leave to a single group. The security group should be tasked with controlling who is authorized to access what, while the network group should be tasked with execution of configuration actions. Typically, the security group should take the task of controlling the logs. With that, it becomes extremely hard for you to perform a misconfiguration on the devices, as in any case it happens, the security group will just detect it in the log files.

6. Secure and verify - all the above actions are very important in detecting any changes made in the network, such as a change in the configuration. If you analyse the traffic contained in the network, you will note any changes made in the policy or any kind of violations to the same.

The status of dynamic data such as the ARP table and routing tables can also be detected. An example of such is the intrusion detection mechanism which can raise an alert in any case a flow is detected in the network but these may not be corresponding to the policy. There are other several mechanisms which can be used for the purpose of detecting anomalies in the network. You can check routing tables for any missing routing prefixes or the ones which might be unknown. The Cisco IOS NetFlow can also be used for the purpose of detecting any misrouted packets.

7. Automation - we recommend that procedures and policies should be automated, specifically the processes which are recurring, since the admin will overlook the details which are contained in the logs and other similar processes. With automated processes, it will also be hard for us to make mistakes, and in case a mistake happens, it will be easy for the admin to detect it, to take the necessary action.

A comprehensive operational security environment is of great significance in any organization, and some security features may require that the organization be of a particular size to take advantage of them. You should always aim to make improvements to the operational processes each time you revisit them, and this is a great step in keeping your network secure. Majority of the parts of the operational processes are very easy for anyone to implement. If you send all the access and the configuration files to a certain single server, and the network operators are not allowed to access, you will have disabled any form of misconfiguration.

Defence in Depth

Most of the operational control functions will not always prevent all the mistakes from occurring. Although they make it hard for a mistake to occur, their great focus is on detecting a mistake once it has occurred. With this, deliberate misconfiguration may be prevented, since no network engineer will accept to do a misconfiguration if they suspect that it can be detected and traced back to him or her. However, avoiding mistakes is hard, and this greatly raises a lot of security concerns.

This is why most organizations opt for extra security measures, and this will help them stay more secure.

If the core of the network is not providing a full separation but you are in need of providing one, maybe because of a misconfiguration, one may choose to implement IPsec. If this is used in the VPN, the separation of VPN will not be broken, because the IPsec has provided it with an additional security. However, when this is done, an additional cost and burden will be incurred, meaning that it comes at an expense. In some organizations, two independent firewalls are implemented, each having a different operational group, so that there will be no single mistake or misconfiguration which will affect the security of the system.

Defense-in-depth refers to employment of different layers of security, and it is a very popular feature in the deployment of network security. However, for this to be done properly, a proper risk analysis has to be conducted. You should have a good understanding about the most popular threats, their impact to the organization, and the costs involved in adding new security layers.

The risk analysis mechanism should help you to know whether the cost of implementing an additional security layer is equal to the cost of the risk if the additional security layer has not been implemented. This will help you to determine whether there is a need for you to implement the extra security layer or do without. However, such analysis should take into account the security counter measures and the network assets. Significant network resources are needed for the risk analysis to be effective.

Complexity and Security

When a network becomes too complex, security violations and operational mistakes become more rampant. This takes into account both the network architecture and the measures which have been put into place for ensuring that there is network security. In terms of security, networks with simple configurations are much preferred.

Similar, the operational management of the network is the same. If the operational procedures become too complex, problems will most likely occur. In such cases, the groups will not be privileged to carry out the emergency operation. If stressed, the security procedures are normally disabled.

The operational model of an organization usually determines how complex an operational policy is. If the support team is much experienced, then the level of complexity will not be equal to that of a team which is just starting up.

The fact is that when you implement additional security measures such as IPsec, they will increase the complexity of your network, and in some other cases, the level of security of the network may be lowered, since the network will have become too complex for maintenance.

Regulation and Compliance

The number of regulations which require operational security procedures to be implemented has improved. As of now, they drive how these operational security procedures are to be implemented.

Chapter 3- Data, Application, and Host Security

Data Security

Multiple cases of stored data being accessed by unauthorized individuals or being damaged have been reported. Securing stored data involves protecting it from unauthorized access, protecting it from damage or destruction either deliberately or accidentally, and protecting it from corruption as well as protecting the data from infection or corruption. Most people are aware of data encryption, and this is one of the technologies which can be implemented for securing data in a tiered architecture.

The following are some measures which can be implemented to ensure that our data is secure:

1. Implement a data protection and security model which is tiered, including multiple rings of perimeter of defence to take care of any applicable threats. If you are using multiple layers, then your data will be more secure as in case one layer is penetrated by attackers, the other security layers will protect the data.

2. Both physical and logical data protection mechanisms should be implemented for protection of data. Physical mechanisms include locking the servers, storage, and the cabinets, while logical data protection mechanisms include authentication, authorization, passwords, and encryption. Data should be stored in a separate cabinet from that used for storing other tools and cabling. For physical security to be a reality, you have to maintain a low profile. In case you are experiencing a power blackout in your area, but you have light in your building, switch off the lights to avoid attracting attention.

With logical security, it is good for you to install a firewall and run the necessary anti-spyware programs and other programs for detecting virus programs in both the network and the data storage servers. For a data storage strategy to be trusted, all the file systems, server operating systems, databases, and applications must be secure to ensure that these are not accessed by unauthorized parties.

3. The door-lock and key-lock combinations should be changed on a regular basis, informing only those who are allowed to access.

4. With some networking tools and storage systems, you are allowed to change the passwords during the first installation of the system. An example of this is the Oracle database. We recommend that you change the default passwords during the process of installation, as attackers might take advantage of them to access your data. Access to the management tools should be restricted to the necessary individuals.

5. Access logs should be leveraged and carry out background checks on the third parties who will be responsible for handling your media and data. In the case of both the fixed and removable data storage media, make sure that you are aware of who has access to them. Identify the weak links in your movement processes of your data and resolve them immediately. You can use data discovery tools to identify some sensitive data in your network which may not be adequately secured.

6. For those transmitting data using electronic means, ensure that the data is kept secure even as it passes through private and public networks. Some mechanisms which can be employed for protecting data in transmission include encryption, IPsec protocol, and Virtual Private networks.

7. Encryption is a good technique for protecting data, both in storage and during transmission. However, the level of encryption will differ from one system to another. It is good for you to determine the level of encryption that you need for your data, and this will be determined by the types of threats that you are facing. The various forms of encryption impact the interoperability of your system with other systems, as well as its performance, so these have to be put into consideration. This will help guide you in the types and level of encryption that you need for your data.

8. Data security should not be allowed to become a bottleneck to the productivity of your system, because this can lead to compromising of the security initiative. If you make the security transparent to those you authorize to use the data, then they will not attempt to overcome your efforts.

9. Data backups and archives should be made very secure, and even

the process of doing the backup or recovery, and the place of storage should be made more secure. You should possess a good understanding of how to unlock the archived data and regulatory compliance.

Host Security

A host represents any computer such as workstations, network servers, laptops, or wirelessly networked devices. Technically, even after securing all of your hosts, there no guarantee exists that the security policies of the organization will be adhered to. In most cases, the users will disclose information to unauthorized parties, and this does not necessarily mean that they will exceed their access privileges or violate their technical measures.

This means that even after ensuring that all our hosts have been adequately secured, we have to implement other measures such as auditing capability and monitoring of network connectivity. These measures are usually implemented in a multi-host environment, rather than from host-to-host.

The following are some security measures which can be taken for securing our hosts:

1. Host-centric - this has to do with the type of operating system which is being used in the host, and the configurations which have been made. It is good for protecting the applications which have been installed in a particular host. However, this mechanism is costly, complex, and it only protects a single host.

2. Controlling access control - this determines the individuals who are authorized to access a particular host. In Unix, three levels of access control exist, which include the following:

• Individual - each user is assigned a unique ID which they used to access the host.
• Group - in Unix, all the users belong to the group "user" by default, but this is in some distros. In others, each user belongs to a singleton group. Different users can belong to the same group.
• World- the host is accessible by anyone.

3. Implementing file permissions - for each directory and file in Unix, it has to be owned by a user, a group, and the world. A set of permission values exist for each level of ownership, which include read, write, and execute.

4. The values for these permissions can be either true, meaning that the permission has been granted, or false. Most directories in Unix should not be writable by the world. If a directory is declared not to be readable to the world, then it means that only the administrator will be in a position to view it. Most directories in Unix should only be writable by the root, which is a good mechanism to ensure that installation of programs into the system without the administrator's consent does not happen. That is why sensitive directories, and especially those which govern how the host functions, have to be owned by the "root" user.

5. Update CMS installations and Scripts
In most cases, most of the attacks to hosts are from malicious users who identify some exploits in the scripts which have been installed into the system. This is why you should ensure that all the CMS which you have installed, together with their add-ons and plugins are kept up-to-date. The good thing is that these can be updated easily, just from the administrative panel.

6. Keep the host passwords updated
Exploited passwords are usually a common source of compromise to the host security. The exploitation can be achieved either through malware installed on the local computer or through brute force attacks.

Brute Force Compromise

In this type of attack, the user tries to guess the host password until they get the correct combination. Most hosts have mechanisms for thwarting brute force attacks, but it is good for you to enhance this by using complex passwords which should be made up of the following characters:

- Uppercase Letters (A-Z)
- Lowercase Letters (a-z)
- Numbers (0-9)
- Special characters (-_.,!^)

Whenever you are updating the host password, you should avoid using any password which had been used earlier before. This is because it will be easy for attackers to compromise your account.

Viruses and Malware

Viruses and other forms of malware programs can be used for stealing your host passwords once they get installed into your system. The malware will work by sniffing the passwords which have been stored in your system as well as the ones which have been stored by FTP. This is why you should perform full malware and virus scans.

7. Creating frequent backups - it is good for you to make frequent backups to ensure that you are safe in case a security compromise occurs.

Application Security Measures

Applications, whether web or desktop, are prone to security attacks. However, web applications are the types of applications which are more vulnerable to security attacks, and hence there is a great need for us to emphasis how to secure these kinds of apps. The following are some measures which can be employed to secure software apps:

1. Content-security policy - when this policy has been implemented, you should turn on alerting, and you will be in a position to identify what is breaking even when you are working on it. Building this retroactively into your website might be somewhat difficult, since one is expected to have as many whitelists as possible, or by creating a massive inventory.

2. X-Frame-Options - it should be put into the block mode and this will help in protecting against click jacking attacks and other forms of framing attacks. Implementation of this can be difficult, since some other sites will begin to frame the site after some time and then use it in that way. It is very painful for you to get each of the sites to update each site linking to you.

3. Running apps with the least privileges - once an application has been executed or run, it will normally run with some privileges on that local computer and maybe on the remote computers. We recommend that you avoid running apps with privileges of being the administrator. Identify the user in the system with the least privileges, and then run the app as that user. Of course, the application will require using some resources in your computer. In such a case, ensure that you set permissions and access controls on such resources. The least permissive setting should be used. The files for your web app should be kept in a folder located below the application root. Users should not be allowed the option of specifying the path to any file access in the application. With this, the users will not be in a position to access the root of your server computer.

4. Know your users - in most cases; sites are anonymously accessed by the users, meaning that there is no need for the users to provide their credentials. In such a case, your application will have to run in the context of a particular user to access the necessary resources.

In the case of intranet applications, they have to be configured to make use of the Windows Integrated Security. With that, the logon credentials of the user can be used for the purpose of accessing the resources. If you need to gather credentials from the user, you should make use of ASP.NET authentication strategies.

5. Protect Against Malicious Input from the User
You should never assume that the input you get from users is safe. Malicious users can send some malicious data from the client to the application. Unfiltered user input should never be echoed. Before you can display entrusted information, echo the HTML, to turn any harmful scripts into strings for display. Unfiltered data should not be stored into the database. If you cannot avoid accepting data in HTML form into the database, make sure that you filter it manually. After filtering, you should then explicitly define what you are going to accept. Avoid creating a filter which will be used for the purpose of filtering malicious data, because it is difficult for anyone to anticipate all malicious input.

6. Cookies should be used securely - with cookies, user-specific data and information can be made readily available. However, since these are to be sent to the browsing computer, they are very vulnerable to malicious use such as spoofing and others. Critical information should never be stored in cookies. This includes information such as a user password, even if you want to store it temporarily. If you notice that something can be spoofed, compromising the security of your application, then avoid storing it in the cookie. What you should do is keep a reference to where the information is located on your local server. Expiration dates for cookies should be set to the shortest time possible. Permanent cookies should be avoided by all means possible. The information contained in cookies should be encrypted.

7. Error messages should be created safely - the kind of error messages displayed by your application can give much information to the malicious user, so you have to be careful with the kind of information you display as an error. Information such as username should not be echoed in the error message, as this can be useful to a malicious user. The errors to be displayed should not be very detailed.

Custom error handling should be used in cases where you suspect that errors will occur.

8. Be careful with Denial-of-service attacks - most attackers compromise your application's security by simply making it unavailable. This can be done by making the app be too busy from servicing other requests or by crashing it. The size limits of user data should be tested first before the storage can be done. File uploads should be governed by a size limit. However, if your application does not have a part for uploading some data or files, do not be worried by this.

The upload limit can be set or configured in the file web.config in the property "maxRequestLength," and the size should be set in kilobytes. Consider the example given below:

```
<configuration>
  <system.web>
    <httpRuntime maxRequestLength="4096" />

  </system.web>
</configuration>
```

9. Sensitive information should be kept safe - sensitive information is the one which needs to be kept safely. Examples of such information include encryption keys and passwords. If this sensitive data is being exchanged between a server computer and the browser, make sure that you use SSL (Secure Socket layer). A protected configuration should be used for securing information which has been stored in configuration files. Sensitive information which must be stored should not be kept in web browsers. Make sure that the encryption techniques that you use are strong enough to safeguard your application.

Chapter 4- Identity Management

This deals with ensuring that only the right individuals access the right resources. This undertaking is very crucial for ensuring that any enterprise is kept secure. The following are some measures which can be taken to manage user identity:

1. Define the individuals who should be allowed to access the resources. These should be employees, consultants and contractors, and even other individuals. If one is authorized to access a particular resource, ensure that they are granted permission to do so.

2. Implement a single system and integrate it - this will provide us with an end-to-end management of the identities throughout the lifecycle that they undergo.

3. Activities should be monitored proactively - this is the easiest way that vulnerabilities can be detected. Any security violations which might have occurred should address effectively, and prevent any unauthorized users from accessing the data or the system.

4. Provide control and knowledge - this should be provided to both the owners of business data and the custodians by making them aware of both permissions and identities. They should have both the visibility and control which is necessary for them to understand what the environment for the organization contains and how they can take control of it.

5. Use a request-and-approval mechanism - this is a good way that changes can be done and then documented. The employees should be allowed to have access to their assigned 5y jobs, and only do what is expected from them, but nothing more. Permissions should always be checked and rechecked to ensure that the right ones are granted to the right users and that no security issues can arise.

6. User account provisioning should be automated - this is a good technique for minimizing errors, improving consistency, and reducing the overhead. With automation, common administrative tasks which seem to be complex can be made much easier. Examples of such tasks include management of passwords and policies in both Linux and Unix systems.

7. Compose compliance rules - these are good, as they will help your organization to adhere to the rules which have been formulated by both the government and other bodies which govern security of systems. With this, you will have helped reduce the burden which is imposed on the IT professionals in your organization, and it is also a good way to ensure that your organization does not violate any rules which have been formulated by the government and industry regarding the security of systems.

8. Manage the roles rather than individuals - there are several ways that any organization can manage access. Some ways include keystroke logging, delegation of granular privileges for the purpose of executing some specific commands, and conducting session audits.

Chapter 5- Cryptography

This is a science which deals with the provision of security to information. Historically, cryptography has been used for the provision of security for communications between government agencies, individuals, and military forces.

Components of Cryptography

In modern cryptography, complex mathematical systems are used together with some other techniques to provide security to our information. Security technologies relying on cryptography for provision of security to both the network and information make use of the following components:

- Encryption algorithms
- Message digest functions
- Hashed Message Authentication Code functions (HMAC)
- Secret key exchange algorithms
- Digital signatures

In Windows 2000, the above components are used for the provision of security by use of the various technologies.

Message Digest Functions

These are also referred to as *"hash functions,"* and they are used for the purpose of generation of digital summaries of information referred to as message digests. The length for message digests ranges between 128 bits to 160 bits, and they are used for provision of a digital identifier for each digital document or file. The message digest functions are mathematical in nature, and they always process information to generate a different message digest for each of the documents. If two documents are identical, then their message digests will also be similar, but a change of a single bit in the document will cause its message digest to change.

You have to note that the message digest will be shorter than the message from which it has been generated, and the digests usually have a finite length; meaning that it is possible for duplicate message digests to exist, a feature known as *"collision."*

However, if the message digest is good and efficient enough, it provides a means to reverse the message digest to get the original data. The fact that a collision can occur does not mean that an attacker can take advantage of it to compromise the security of data and network.

Message digests are usually used together with the public key technology for creation of digital signatures which are usually employed in integrity, non-repudiation, and authentication of users of a system or network. The digital signing technology makes use of the message digests to provide the integrity in data contained in electronic documents and files.

This technology is widely employed when sending e-mails. The complete email is changed into a message digest, signed digitally by use of the private key of the sender, and then this is transmitted together with the email message. For the recipient of the message to check for its integrity, they can do the following:

1. Compute the digest for the message by use of a similar digest function.
2. Use the public key of the sender for verification of the signed message digest.
3. The new message digest will then be compared to the original one.

If the two message digests fail to match, then the recipient will deduce that the message was altered during transmission, and that the message is not reliable.

Digital Signatures

Digital signatures are used for identifying electronic identities for any online transactions. The signature will identify the sender of a message which has been signed digitally, and the integrity of the signed data will be ensured by protecting it from corruption or from any form of interference.

A simple way to create a digital signature is by encryption of the data using the private key of the sender on the originator's side, and then enclosing the signature by use of the original data. Anybody has the public key of the originator will be in a position to decrypt the signature and then perform a comparison between the original message and the one they have received. If the messages match, then it will be free of interference, but in case of a match, the message will have been corrupted during transmission. In case an attacker intrudes the message during transmission, it will be hard for them to create a new and valid signature.

Secret Key Exchange

If you need secret key cryptography to work effectively during online communications, the secret has to be shared securely with the necessary parties and then protected from being known and used by any unauthorized parties. There are algorithms which are used for the purpose of exchanging the secret keys in computing, and an example of such an algorithm is the RSA key exchange.

Encryption

This is the process of coding your plaintext for creation of cipher text, and the process of decoding the cipher text to get the plaintext is referred to as *"decryption."* In modern technologies, mathematical keys and digital keys are used for the purpose of carrying out both encryption and decryption.

Hashed Message Authentication

This is a function for authenticating messages which are passed during Internet communications. This is widely used by the technologies dealing with Internet security such as the IPsec and TLS protocols.

Conclusion

We have come to the conclusion of this guide. Security is very important when it comes to the computer network, data, and applications. There is a need for us to ensure that these are well secured. There are various forms of threats to network security. Examples of these include viruses, worms, Trojan horses, and others. Each of these affects the network in a different and unique way, but some are related in terms of their functionality.

There are security measures which can be taken to ensure that the network is kept safe from the above forms of attacks. These have been discussed in this guide, and there is a need for any organization to implement those measures to be secure. Attackers also have numerous ways which they can use to attack the computer network of an organization. For instance, with the growth in technology and the Internet, numerous tools have been created, and these can help attackers carry out malicious activities to the computer network of an organization. Data in transmission over the computer network should be kept private and confidential, meaning that it should not get into the hands of unauthorized personnel.

Most organizations need to protect their sensitive data from getting into the hands of some individuals such as their competitors, enemies, or the public. Several measures can be taken to ensure that this is achieved, and these have been discussed in the guide. The identity of users who access the systems of an organization is very important. Mechanisms should be implemented to ensure that a user accesses what they are supposed to access, but what they aren't supposed to access. With such mechanisms, the organization's data will be kept safe and secure.

www.ingramcontent.com/pod-product-compliance
Lightning Source LLC
Chambersburg PA
CBHW052144070326
40689CB00051B/3653